ESSENTIAL DK COMPUTERS

INTERNET

FLASH
AN INTRODUCTION

KU-207-985

ABOUT THIS BOOK

Flash: An Introduction is an easy-to-use guide to a powerful software program that enables you to create animations and interactivity that will revolutionize your website.

WEB BUILDING WITH PROGRAMS such as Macromedia's Dreamweaver has never been easier, but the next step of adding animated elements can appear daunting. This book is intended for those web builders who want to take that step, and it offers a complete guide to the basic functions that Flash has to offer.

The first chapter provides an overview of what Flash can do for you, and this is followed by a chapter on creating graphics in Flash. The next two chapters show you how to produce animation and interactivity for your website, featuring techniques for rollovers and animated buttons onscreen.

Finally you are shown how to convert your Flash movies into Shockwave Flash files that can be uploaded to the web.

The chapters and the subsections present the information using step-by-step

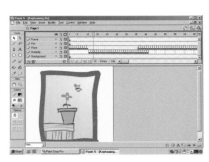

sequences. Virtually every step is accompanied by an illustration showing how your screen should look at each stage.

The book contains several features to help you understand both what is happening and what you need to do.

Command keys, such as ENTER and CTRL, are shown in these rectangles: Enter↵ and Ctrl, so that there's no confusion, for example, over whether you should press that key or type the letters "ctrl."

Cross-references are shown in the text as left- or right-hand page icons: ⌐ and ⌐. The page number and the reference are shown at the foot of the page.

As well as the step-by-step sections, there are boxes that explain particular features in detail, and tip boxes that provide alternative methods. Finally, at the back, you will find a glossary of common terms and a comprehensive index.

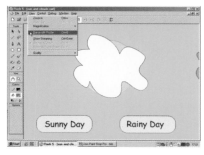

ESSENTIAL DK COMPUTERS

I N T E R N E T

FLASH
AN INTRODUCTION

K A T E   W I L L I A M S

**LONDON, NEW YORK, MUNICH,
MELBOURNE, DELHI**

Senior Editor Amy Corzine
Senior Art Editor Sarah Cowley
DTP Designer Julian Dams
Production Controller Michelle Thomas

Managing Editor Adèle Hayward
Senior Managing Art Editor Nigel Duffield

Produced for Dorling Kindersley Limited by
Design Revolution Limited, Queens Park Villa,
30 West Drive, Brighton, East Sussex BN2 2GE
Editorial Director Ian Whitelaw
Senior Designer Andrew Easton
Project Editor Julie Whitaker
Designer Paul Bowler

First published in Great Britain in 2001 by
Dorling Kindersley Limited,
80 Strand, London WC2R 0RL

A Penguin Company

2 4 6 8 10 9 7 5 3 1

A CIP catalogue record for this book is available from the British Library.

ISBN 0-7513-3583-5

Colour reproduced by Colourscan, Singapore
Printed and bound in Italy by Graphicom

For our complete catalogue visit
www.dk.com

CONTENTS

FLASH ESSENTIALS

Macromedia's Flash enables you to create lively animation and stimulating interactivity for the web, with the added advantage of fast download times.

WHAT CAN FLASH DO?

If you want to add movement, sound, and interactivity to a web site, then Flash is the tool for you. Flash can be used to create animated movies to embed into a web page, or, if you prefer, you can start from scratch and design a whole interactive site in Flash. But dynamic content does not have to lead to slow download times, as the vector nature of Flash reduces file sizes dramatically. What this means is that Flash stores shapes and lines as mathematical formulae rather than saving information about the position and color of every dot or pixel, as bitmap programs do. Flash movies deliver even faster over the web because they are streamed to your computer, so the movie starts to play from the first frame before the later frames have even arrived. This all adds up to a powerful tool for creating fast and stimulating web content.

WHAT IS A FLASH MOVIE?

Each project file you open is a Flash Movie. It can contain colorful images that are created by using Flash's drawing tools and others you have imported. You can animate these images, make them interactive, and add a soundtrack. The finished project can then be published for the web or as a stand-alone movie.

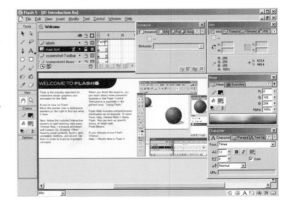

OPENING AND PLAYING A MOVIE

To get some sense of what Flash can do, you are going to open and play a sample movie. First, go to **File** in the menu bar.

Choose **Open** from the drop-down menu. From the **Look in:** drop-down panel, navigate to **Local Disk** (C:).

1 OPENING A MOVIE

● Double click on the **Program Files** folder. Navigate through the **Macromedia** folder, into the **Flash 5** folder, and then to **Samples**.
● Select **Keyframing.fla** and click **Open**.

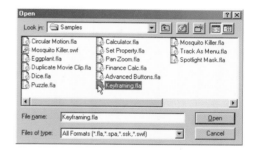

2 PLAYING A MOVIE

● Click on **Control** in the menu bar and choose **Play** from the drop-down menu. Then, sit back and watch the animation.

A quick way to play and stop

Use the [Enter] key as a keyboard shortcut to play and stop a Flash movie. When viewing a Flash movie, it can be stopped and restarted in any frame.

THE FLASH INTERFACE

If your panels are set to their default layout, the Flash window will look like this when you first open a new, blank movie. The key features are the stage, the timeline, the toolbox, and the floating panels. With all the panels open, the screen will be rather cluttered, but they can be closed and opened when necessary. To make a new movie, choose **New** from the **File** drop-down menu. You do not have to close the current movie to do this because Flash lets you have several movies open at once.

THE FLASH WINDOW

❶ Work Area
You can place movie elements in the work area and bring them into your animation when needed. You can think of the Work Area as backstage.

❷ Toolbox
This contains the drawing, selection, color, and view tools, and their options.

❸ Menu Bar
This allows you to access the drop-down menus as in other Windows programs.

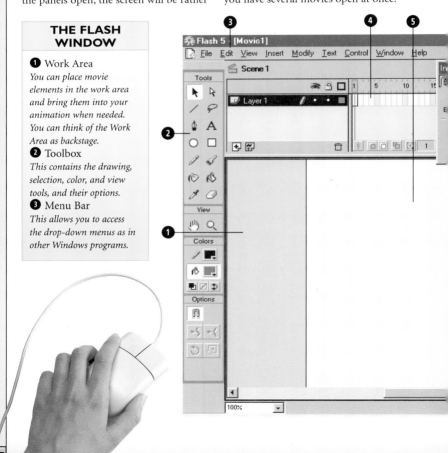

THE FLASH INTERFACE · 9

SETTING THE PANELS TO DEFAULT LAYOUT

To set the floating panels to Flash's default layout, first go to **Window** in the main menu. From the **Window** drop-down menu, choose **Panel Sets** and then **Default Layout** from the sub-menu.

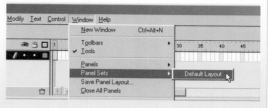

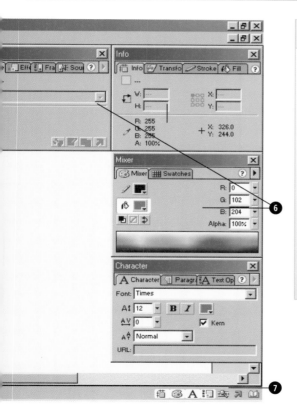

THE FLASH WINDOW

4 Timeline
You create your animations through frames and keyframes in the timeline.

5 Stage
This is the area where your movie is displayed.

6 Panels
There are so many floating panels that you should only open the ones you need. The panels allow you to edit elements of your movie, and each has a specialist job.

7 Launcher Bar
This gives you a quick and easy way to open and close the common panels.

WORKING WITH PANELS

Flash's floating panels allow you to control the appearance or behavior of a large number of elements in your movie. For example, you can choose a font face, pick a color to fill a shape, or change the thickness of an outline in the various panels. You will learn to use a lot of these functions later in the book, but at this stage it is important to be able to organize your panels on the screen.

1 CLOSING AND OPENING PANELS

● To try the first method, click on the Character icon in the launcher bar to close the **Character** panel.
● Click on the **Character** icon again to reopen the **Character** panel.

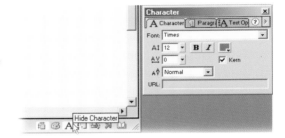

● To use the second method, go to the **Window** drop-down menu, select **Panels**, and the Panels menu will appear. Note that any open panels will show a check mark in the Panels menu.
● Here, click on **Info** to close the panel.
● Repeat this sequence to reopen the **Info** panel.

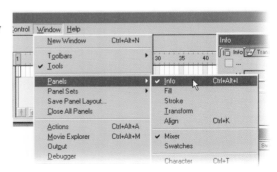

● Click on the **Close** box
indicator (the **x**) in the top
right corner of the **Instance**
Panel window.
● Note that the **Instance**
icon is now deselected on
the launcher bar.

Instance icon is now deselected ●

2 MOVING PANELS

● Click and drag on a
panel's blue bar to
reposition it.

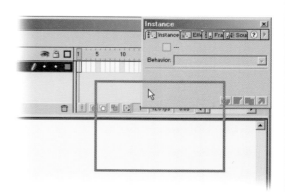

3 SAVING SPACE

● To keep the desktop tidy,
panel windows can be
stacked on top of each other.
● The **Info**, **Mixer**, **Instance**,
and **Character** panels each
contain up to four other
panels. To bring the panel
you want to use to the
front, click on its tab.

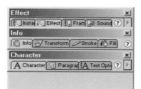

INTRODUCING THE TIMELINE

The timeline is central to making Flash movies. It allows you to build up the frames of your movie, including keyframes, which represent moments of change; coordinate movement, sound, and interactivity within the film itself; organize elements into layers; and move backward and forward through your movie. In order to analyze the timeline more closely, the example we are using here is a movie that uses frames, keyframes, and layers. We will start with **Keyframing.fla,** which should still be open.

1 SELECTING KEYFRAMING.FLA

● Go to the **Window** drop-down menu and click on **Keyframing.fla** at the bottom. If Keyframing.fla is not listed, open as before.

Moving the timeline
To undock the timeline from the top menu bar, click and drag it away. As a floating window, it can be redocked to any of the screen borders by dragging it there.

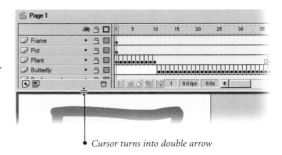

2 RESIZING THE TIMELINE

● You can resize the timeline to display more layers or more of the stage.
● Place the cursor at the base of the timeline, and it turns into a double arrow.
● Click and drag until the timeline is the size you require.

● *Cursor turns into double arrow*

7 **Opening a Movie**

EXPLORING THE TIMELINE

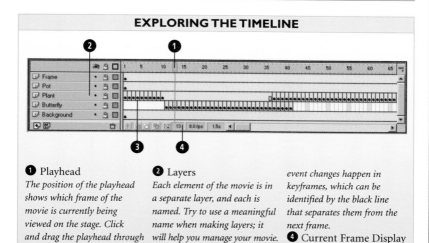

① Playhead
The position of the playhead shows which frame of the movie is currently being viewed on the stage. Click and drag the playhead through the movie manually and note that the current frame number displays changes.

② Layers
Each element of the movie is in a separate layer, and each is named. Try to use a meaningful name when making layers; it will help you manage your movie.

③ Frames and Keyframes
A Flash movie is made up of frames and keyframes. Major

event changes happen in keyframes, which can be identified by the black line that separates them from the next frame.

④ Current Frame Display
This indicates the number of the frame currently showing on the stage.

MODIFYING THE STAGE

The stage is the place where the movie is displayed in Flash. You can control and modify various aspects of the stage, such as the size, background color, and frame rate, with the **Movie Properties** box.

A small stage is more appropriate for a Flash element that is to be embedded in a web page, whereas a full screen stage would be used for making an entire web page in Flash.

1 CHANGING THE FRAME RATE
● Go to the **Modify** drop-down menu and choose **Movie**. This will give you the **Movie Properties** box.

● The default frame rate
is 12 frames per second,
but you can type in a new
value if you wish.
● A lower frame rate will
save file size, but will make
a less smooth movie.

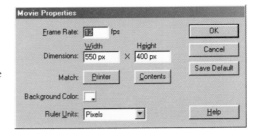

2 RESIZING THE STAGE

● The default stage size
is 550 x 400 pixels, but you
can enter new values for
width and height in the
Dimensions field of the
Movie Properties box.

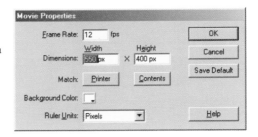

3 PICKING A STAGE COLOR

● Click on the **Background
Color** field in the **Movie
Properties** box to see the
color palette.
● The cursor becomes
an eyedropper, which you
can use to pick your choice
of background color for
the stage.
● Click on **OK** to apply.

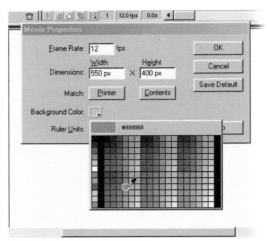

4 SHOWING THE GRID

● The grid is useful for positioning elements evenly on the stage. It will not be present in your finished movie.

● To switch on the grid, go to the **View** drop-down menu, choose **Grid**, then **Show Grid**.

● **Snap to Grid** makes the lines in the grid act like magnets.

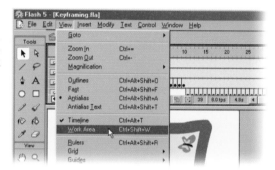

5 ACTIVATING THE WORK AREA

● You can switch the work area off and on by going to the **View** drop-down menu and selecting **Work Area**.

6 DISPLAYING MAIN MENU ICONS

● The main menu icons can be turned on and off by going to **Window** and selecting **Toolbars** and then **Main** from the drop-down menus.

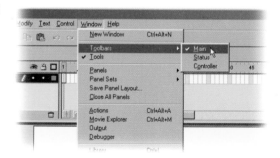

DESIGNING GRAPHICS

Flash will allow you to draw, paint, and color original artwork using tools from the toolbox. To explore the toolbox, hold the cursor over a tool and a box pops up showing its name.

WHAT'S IN THE TOOLBOX?

There are four sections in the toolbox. **Tools** contains the important drawing, coloring, and selection tools; the **View** tools change the stage's view; the **Color** section allows you to edit colors; and the **Options** vary depending on the tool selected.

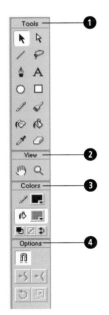

THE TOOLBOX

❶ Tools
The Arrow, Subselect, and Lasso are selection tools. The Line, Pen, Pencil, and Brush are line drawing tools. The Pen, Oval, and Rectangle are shape drawing tools. Finally, the Paint Bucket, Ink Bottle, and Dropper are coloring tools.

❷ View
You can zoom in or out by selecting the Zoom Tool. You can also Enlarge or Reduce in the Zoom Tool Options. The Hand Tool allows you to move the stage around the screen when you click and drag.

❸ Colors
Choose Fill and Stroke colors in this section of the toolbox.

❹ Options
Look at the different Options offered by the various tools. Some of the tools have further properties that can be modified in panels.

Moving the toolbox
The default position of the toolbox is docked on the left of the screen, but it can be undocked and left floating or it can be dragged to the other edges of the screen.

DRAWING AND COLORING SHAPES

A quick and easy way to draw geometric shapes is to use the **Oval** and **Rectangle** tools. To make a perfect circle or square, hold down the ⇧ Shift key as you draw your shape. Use the **Paint Bucket** and **Ink Bottle** to change colors.

1 DRAWING A RECTANGLE

● Pick up the **Rectangle** 🖰 from the toolbox.

● Click and drag the cursor across the stage.

● Note that the fill and stroke colors of the graphic match the colors displayed in the toolbox.

2 CHANGING THE FILL COLOR

● Click on the **Fill Color** 🖰 icon in the toolbox to see its color palette.

● Move the cursor, which is now a dropper, to a new color and click.

● Pick up the **Paint Bucket** 🖰 from the toolbox, drag it to your graphic, and click on it to change its color.

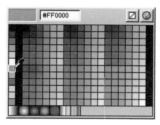

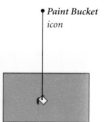

Paint Bucket icon

Fills and strokes

In Flash, a fill is the color or pattern that makes up the body of a shape. A stroke is a shape's outline.

3 CHANGING THE OUTLINE SETTINGS

● Go to **Window**, choose **Panels** from the drop-down menu, then **Stroke** to access the **Stroke** panel.
● To change the outline color, click on the **Stroke color** box.

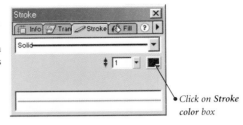

*Click on **Stroke** color box*

● To pick up a new color, click on the selected color with the dropper.

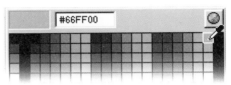

● To change the style of the outline, click on the **Stroke style** arrow and pick a new line style.
● To change the outline thickness, click on the **Stroke height** arrow and slide the pointer to the required level.

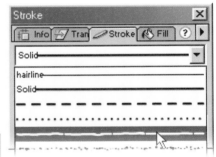

UNABLE TO FILL YOUR SHAPE?

If you cannot get your **Paint Bucket** to fill a shape, there may be a gap in the stroke. You can change the **Gap Size** from **Options** in the toolbox to **Close Small, Medium,** or **Large Gaps** so Flash will fill an outline with a hole in it.

4 APPLYING THE NEW OUTLINE

● Select the **Ink Bottle** from the toolbox.
● Your cursor will become an ink bottle.
● Click on the rectangle to apply the new outline settings.

Click on the Ink Bottle ●

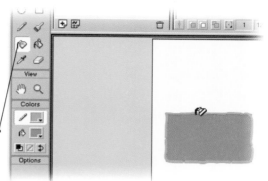

SELECTING A SHAPE

You have to be careful when making selections in Flash because fills and strokes are separate elements in a graphic.

Using a variety of tools and methods, you can select part of an object, a whole object, or several objects at once.

1 SELECTING A FILL

● Select the **Arrow** tool from the toolbox.
● Click on the fill within your shape.
● Note that it now shows a pattern within the fill.

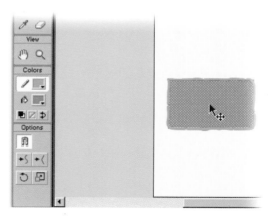

2 MOVING A FILL

● Click and drag the fill away from the stroke.
● To undo, go to **Edit** in the main menu and select **Undo**. You can edit/undo up to 100 times, which allows plenty of scope for stepping back through your work to fix any errors.

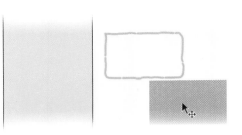

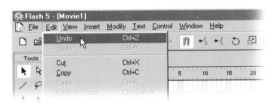

3 SELECTING BOTH FILL AND STROKE

● Double click on your shape to select both fill and stroke.
● Note that a pattern appears again, but this time it covers the stroke as well as the fill.
● Press [Esc] on the keyboard to deselect.
● Alternatively, select the **Arrow** tool from the toolbox. Click and drag the **Arrow** tool around your shape to select all.

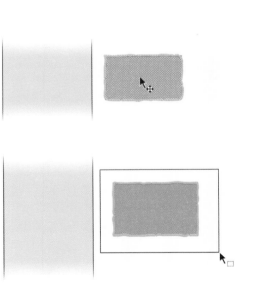

4 SELECTING MULTIPLE OBJECTS

● When you want to select odd shapes or objects that are unevenly spaced,

you need to choose the **Lasso** tool.

● Next, drag the cursor around the chosen graphics in order to select them.

● To make the lasso draw straight lines, click on **Polygon Mode** in the **Options** section at the bottom of the toolbox.

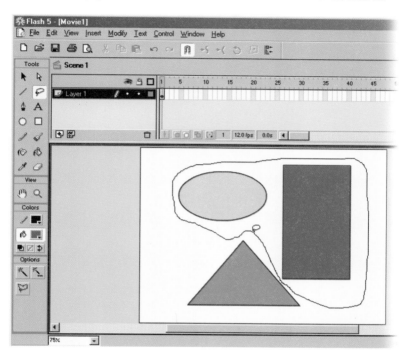

GROUPING GRAPHICS

You can make a fill and stroke behave as a single element by grouping them together. With the whole graphic highlighted, go to **Modify**. From the drop-down menu, select **Group**. If you want to edit the elements separately, you can ungroup them again from the Modify menu.

3-D EFFECTS

On some occasions, you may wish to create a 3-D effect with your graphics. A gradient fill can be useful for creating 3-D effects around objects. Here, you will draw a sphere to show the stunning effects that can be achieved with 3-D.

1 SELECTING THE COLORS
● Select the **Oval** tool from the toolbox.
● Then, select **Stroke Color** and click on the **No Color** option.

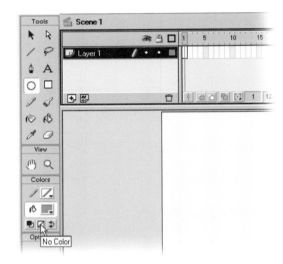

● Click the **Fill Color** box to select its color palette.
● Choose a radial gradient from the bottom of the palette.

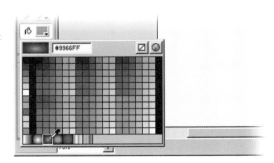

2 DRAWING THE SPHERE

● Hold the ⟨⇧ Shift⟩ key down as you drag across your stage to draw your sphere.

● Select the **Paint Bucket** from the toolbox.

● Note that the fill color is still the radial gradient that you chose before.

● Click off center on your ball to move the center of the gradient fill. This improves the 3-D effect.

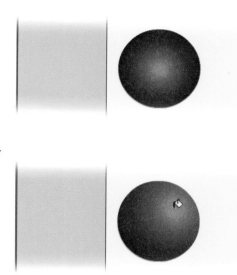

USING THE ERASER

The **Erase** tool has options that allow you to choose which part of your graphic will be erased when you click and drag across it.

● Select the **Erase** tool from the toolbox.

● Click on the **Erase Mode** options to see the choices.

● **Erase Normal** will erase everything, or you can choose an option that restricts the area to be erased.

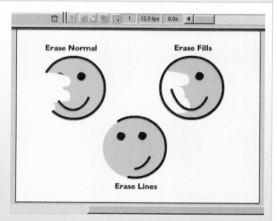

WORKING WITH LAYERS

So far, you have been dealing with small numbers of very simple graphics, but Flash movies can have a lot of artwork on the stage at once. These more complex Flash movies arrange the separate graphical elements in layers, which is like having each piece of artwork on a clear sheet of acetate stacked on top of each other. This allows you to move, edit, or delete any individual element within the movie without it affecting the rest of the movie, and also avoids the problem of deleting and splitting graphics that share a layer.

1 LOOKING AT MULTIPLE OBJECTS

● This example has three shapes that overlap on the stage in one layer.
● Select and move the triangle. Note that it has erased the parts of the graphics that were underneath.

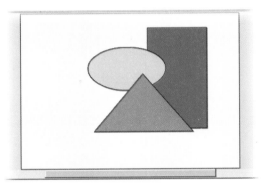

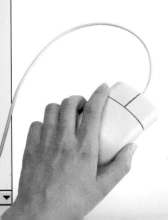

2 NAMING THE FIRST LAYER

● To make a new Flash movie, go to **File** and select **New** from the drop-down menu.

● Draw an oval on the empty stage by selecting the **Oval** tool and dragging the cursor across the stage.

● Double click on the **Layer Name** in the time-line, which is currently called **Layer 1**.

● Type in the name **Oval** and press [Enter ←] on the keyboard.

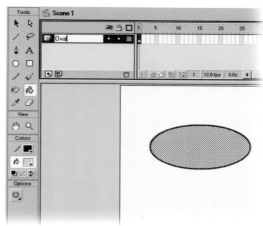

3 MAKING THE SECOND LAYER

● Click on the **Insert Layer** icon, which is the plus sign on the bottom left of the timeline.

● A new layer called **Layer 2** appears in the timeline above **Oval**.

● Double click on the **Layer Name** for **Layer 2**.

● Type in the name **Rectangle** and press [Enter ←] on the keyboard.

● Note that the first frame in the **Oval** layer has a black dot in it, showing that the movie contains artwork in that frame, and that the first frame in the **Rectangle** layer is empty.

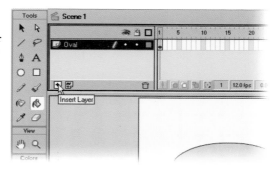

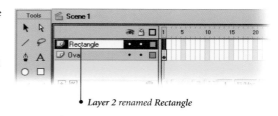

● *Layer 2 renamed Rectangle*

❶ **Tools**

4 GRAPHIC ON THE SECOND LAYER

● Select the **Rectangle** by clicking on the **Layer Name** in the timeline.

● The selected layer has a black background and a white name. It also has a pencil icon in its **Layer Name** bar.

● Pick up the **Rectangle** tool and draw a rectangle overlapping the oval.

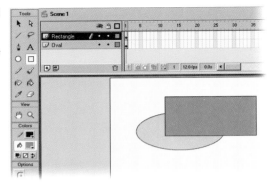

5 CHANGING THE STACKING

● Select the **Oval** layer by clicking its **Layer Name** bar.

● Click and hold as you drag the **Oval** layer into a new position above the **Rectangle** layer.

● As you drop the layer into its new position, you will see that the oval graphic appears above the rectangle graphic on the timeline.

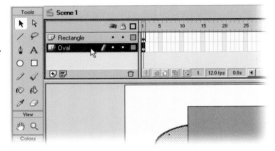

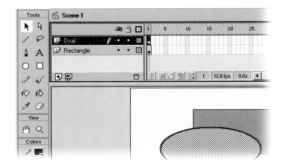

6 MOVING A GRAPHIC

- With the **Oval** layer and the oval graphic selected, use the **Arrow** tool to drag the graphics apart.
- Note that graphics on separate layers do not delete areas of overlap.

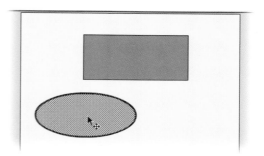

DRAWING LINES

When making Flash graphics, you do not always want to make solid, even shapes, so Flash offers tools for drawing lines and uneven shapes. You can make straight lines or curves, and draw freehand with the **Line**, **Pencil**, **Brush**, and **Pen** tools.

1 DRAWING WITH THE PENCIL

- Pick up the **Pencil** tool from the toolbox.
- Click on **Pencil Mode** in **Options** and choose **Smooth**.

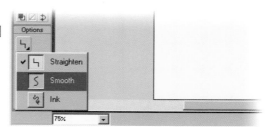

ORGANIZING YOUR FLASH MOVIE

As your Flash movie project becomes more complex, you will soon become confused if you do not name the layers in a logical way. You might know now that the layer called Button 1 contains the blue button and Button 2 the red one, but to avoid having to remind yourself later, name them "Blue Button" and "Red Button" from the start.

---

 ❶ Tools

 ❹ Options

● Draw a curved line across the stage by clicking and dragging the mouse.
● When you release the mouse, you will see the line smooth out.
● If you wish to edit the color, thickness, and line style of the pencil, go to the **Stroke** panel.
● **Straighten Mode** straightens out kinks in lines and **Ink** allows you to keep your freehand style.

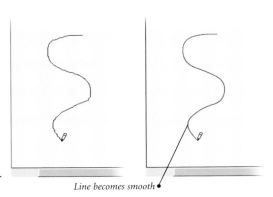

Line becomes smooth ●

2 PAINTING WITH THE BRUSH

● Select the **Brush** tool from the toolbox.
● Choose a color of paint from the **Fill Color** dropdown menu.
● You can change the size and shape of the brush from the **Options** section.

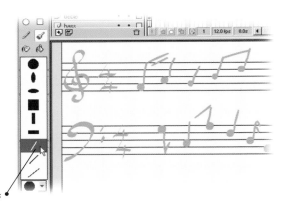

Brush shape options ●

WHERE CAN I PAINT?

Like the **Eraser**, the **Brush** tool has a **Brush Mode** menu in its **Options**, which allows you to choose where the paintbrush will work. You can paint anywhere on the stage in **Paint Normal Mode**, or you can restrict the paintbrush to **Fills**, **Behind**, **Selections**, and **Inside**. Experiment with these settings until you get the desired effect.

| 18 | **Changing the Outline Settings** |

3 STRAIGHT LINES WITH THE PEN

● Pick up the **Pen** tool from the toolbox.

● The cursor has now become the pen tip. Note that a small cross appears beside it – this signifies that you can create the starting point for a line.

● Click and release on the stage.

● Move the cursor to another point and click again.

● A line set to the current **Stroke** panel attributes will join these two points.

4 ANGULAR SHAPES WITH THE PEN

● Click another point on the stage and the **Pen** tool will join the points again.

● Continue to make lines as sides of a shape and work toward the original starting point.

● If you hold [Shift] as you click, this will constrain the angle between the lines to 45 or 90 degrees.

● As you move the cursor over the original point, a small circle will appear. Click to complete your shape.

● You will see that it fills with the currently selected fill color.

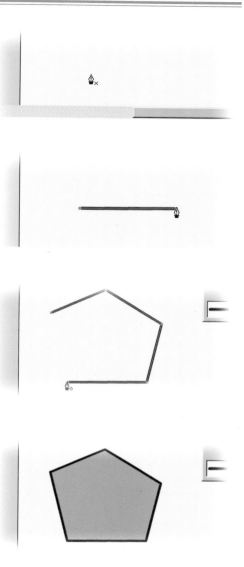

5 MAKING CURVES WITH THE PEN

● Go to **File** and select **New** to make a new movie.

● Select the **Pen** tool, click and drag on the stage, then release.

● The guideline that you create is the starting point of a curve.

● The direction in which you drag the cursor will dictate the direction of the curve; the length of the line will dictate the depth of the curve.

● Click and drag a second guideline on the stage.

● A curved line appears along the path between the center points of the two guidelines.

6 MAKING CURVED SHAPES

● Make a third guideline to add another side to the curved shape.

● Continue to make curves and work toward the original starting point.

● When the small circle appears by the pen cursor, click on the starting point to complete the shape.

● If you want to complete the shape before reaching the starting point, double click on any point.

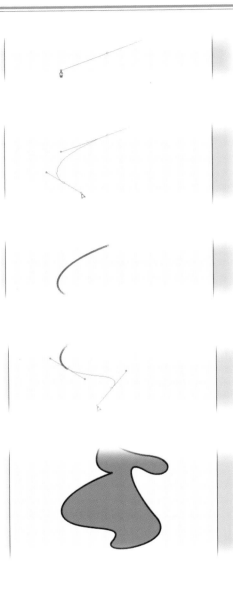

WORKING WITH TEXT

The **Text** tool, found in the toolbox, is one of the most useful features in Flash graphics because it is used so frequently to make such things as headings, buttons, labels, captions, and entire paragraphs of information. Text can also be animated to good effect in a Flash movie, as we will see in a later chapter .

1 SELECTING TEXT ATTRIBUTES

● Select the **Text** tool from the toolbox.

● Open the **Character** panel by clicking on the character icon in the Launcher Bar. Alternatively, go to **Window** on the menu bar and select **Panels**, then **Character** from the drop-down menu .

● To choose a font face, click on the **Font** arrow in the **Character** Panel and select a font from the list.

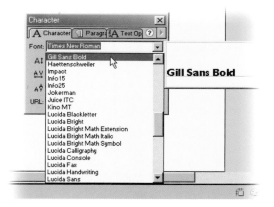

● To change the font size, click on the **Font height** arrow in the **Character** panel and slide the pointer to the required level.

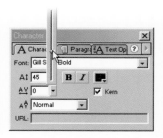

Smoothing Text

If text appears jagged, go to **View** and select **Antialias Text** from the drop-down menu. This will make it smoother.

| 42 | **Creating Text to Animate** |

| 10 | **Working with Panels** |

● To pick a font color, click on the **Text (fill) color** box in the **Character** panel and use the dropper to select a color.

Text (fill) color box ●

Text color box ●

2 SINGLE LINES OF TEXT

● Click on the stage and type in your text.
● Note how the text field expands to accommodate the text on a single line.
● When the text field is a single line, its resize handle on the top right is a circle.

Resize handle ●

> **Working with Flash Text**

3 FIXED WIDTH TEXT FIELDS

● Take the cursor over the circular resize handle; it will become a double arrow.
● Click and drag the resize handle to the left.
● The resize box now displays as a square.
● The text box now has a fixed width, but it will expand downward to accommodate any more text that you type.

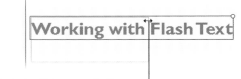

Resize handle becomes a double-arrow ●

The resize box is now a square ●

USING IMAGES FROM OUTSIDE FLASH

You can create great-looking Flash movies using the tools provided in Flash's toolbox, but sometimes you need to use an external image – for example, a photo. Be aware, however, that photos are bitmaps and have a much larger file size than graphics created in Flash. A Flash movie containing a lot of photos or other images created in bitmap graphics programs can be slow to download.

IMPORTING IMAGES FROM OUTSIDE

● Go to **File** menu and select **Import** from the drop-down menu.

● Go to the folder where you have saved the image, select it, and click on **Open**.

● The image appears on the stage, where it can be used like any other graphic in Flash.

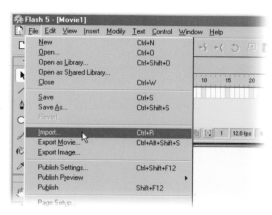

CREATING ANIMATION

Animation is where Flash comes into its own. The ability to make dynamic web pages, using a number of different techniques, is what really makes Flash stand out.

HOW DO ANIMATIONS WORK?

The graphics created so far have been in the first frame. Movement is created by adding more frames and changing the appearance or position of graphics across those frames. Major changes occur in keyframes, which can be identified in the timeline by the black line that separates one keyframe from the next frame.

FLASH ANIMATION TECHNIQUES

The techniques for creating animation in Flash are either frame-by-frame animation, in which every frame is a keyframe, or Tweening, in which keyframes are beginning and end points, with Flash filling in the intervening frames.

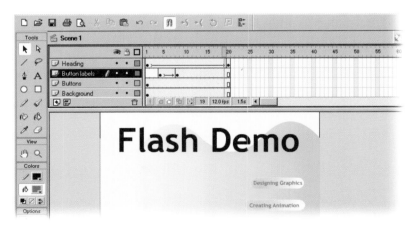

FRAME-BY-FRAME ANIMATION

This example creates a frame-by-frame animation in just two keyframes. If you want to create your own version of this exercise, use the techniques developed in the section on Designing Graphics (see page 16) to recreate the warning sign.

1 INSERTING A NEW KEYFRAME

● At the start of the exercise, the graphics are in one frame and one layer only.

● Right mouse click on the required frame, in this case frame two, to see the Frame menu.

● Select **Insert Keyframe** from the drop-down menu.

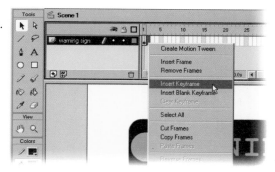

DRAWING A ROUND EDGED RECTANGLE

To make a rectangle with soft, rounded corners, select the **Rectangle** tool, then go to the **Round Rectangle Radius** icon in the **Options** toolbox. Try experimenting with different **Corner Radius** figures, (accessed in the **Rectangle Settings** pop-up box) – the higher the number, the more rounded the shape.

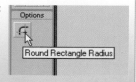

● A new keyframe contains a copy of all the graphics from the previous keyframe in that layer.

● The graphics will be selected in a new keyframe, so press [Esc] on your keyboard to deselect.

• *The new keyframe*

2 EDITING THE IMAGE

● Pick up the **Paint Bucket** tool, click on the **Fill Color** box and use the dropper to select yellow.

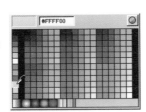

● Make sure the playhead is on frame two in the timeline, and click the **Paint Bucket** on the right circle to make it yellow.

The playhead is in frame two

Click on the right button •

● Pull the playhead back to frame one.

● Click the **Paint Bucket** on the left circle to make it yellow.

3 PLAYING THE ANIMATION

● Go to **Control** in the main menu bar and select **Loop Playback** from the drop-down menu.

● Press [Enter ↵] or [↵] on the keyboard to play the animation.

● Note how the playhead moves on the timeline. In **Loop Playback**, Flash will play a movie from the first frame to the last, then start again. In this case, there are only two frames in the movie, so the Flash playhead continually jumps backward and forward.

● The lights are flashing too fast, so press [Enter ↵] or [↵] again to stop the animation before fixing the problem.

Flash playhead jumps back and forth

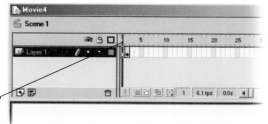

4 CHANGING THE FRAME RATE

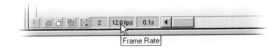

● Double click on the **Frame Rate** in the timeline to access the **Movie Properties** box.

● Type **6** in the **Frame Rate** box and click **OK**.

● Play the animation again. It now plays at half the speed (six frames per second instead of 12).

Change the frame rate ●

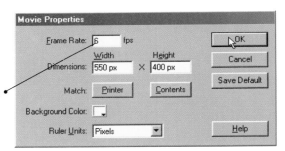

5 SAVING THE MOVIE

● Use **File** and **Save As** to save the Flash movie. Browse to a folder of your choice, name the movie, and **Save**.

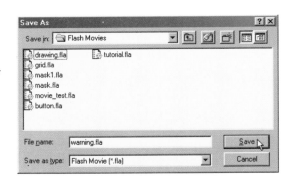

FILE TYPES

The file type is a Flash movie file, and has the extension **.fla**. This is the format you need to use while working on a Flash project, but it is not the format that you will use to publish your Flash movie on the web. Finished movies are output in the Shock- wave Flash format, and have the extension **.swf**. This is covered in the section on publishing movies on the web ⌐.

Publishing for the Web
68

MOTION TWEENING

For frame-by-frame animation, you must create or edit artwork for every frame of your movie, which can be a laborious process. Flash offers a simpler method of creating movement, called Motion Tweening. If two keyframes that are not in adjacent frames contain the same artwork in different positions on the stage, Flash can fill in the intervening frames and create smooth motion between these two points. Not only is this form of animation quicker and easier to create, it also reduces the size of files and therefore download times. However, to perform Motion Tweening, you must convert your graphics into reusable symbols.

1 CONVERTING TO SYMBOLS

● Draw a ball in the **Work Area** to the left of the stage. You can use the methods covered in Designing Graphics to create the ball.
● Pick up the **Arrow** tool and select the artwork by double clicking on it.
● Go to **Insert** on the main menu bar and select **Convert to Symbol** from the drop-down menu.

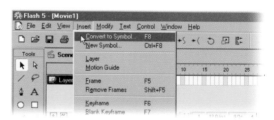

● In the **Symbol Properties** box, go to the **Behavior** options and select **Graphic**.

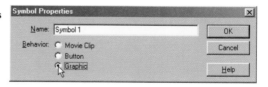

3-D Effects

● Give the Symbol an appropriate name (we have called it **Blue Ball**) and click on **OK**.

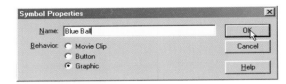

● Note that the artwork now displays inside a boundary when it is selected rather than in a checkered pattern. It can no longer be edited on the stage.

2 CREATING A MOTION TWEEN

● Right mouse click in frame 12 to access the **Frame** menu.
● Select **Insert Keyframe** (frame one of the layer was automatically a keyframe).

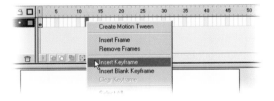

● With this new keyframe selected in the timeline, drag the ball to the **Work Area** to the right of the stage.

● The ball will be in this position only in frame 12.

● Frames 1–11 still display the graphic from frame one, which is the first keyframe.
● Right mouse click on any of the frames between one and 12 to access the **Frame** menu.
● Select **Create Motion Tween**.
● An arrow will appear between the two keyframes in the timeline.
● Play the animation by pressing [Enter ↵] or [↵] on the keyboard. The ball will move across the stage.

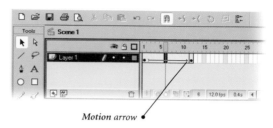

Motion arrow ●

3 ANIMATING IN LAYERS

● Animations can be made more complex by having several objects move across the stage at once,

but every object animated with a Tween must be in a layer of its own.
● Make a new layer ⬜ and a second ball animation, but this time insert the first

keyframe at frame five and the second at frame 20.
● The animations have been staggered by the positioning of the start and end point keyframes.

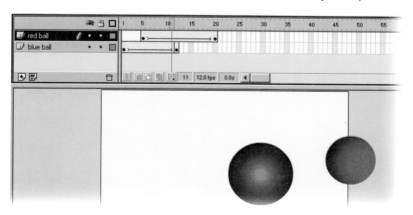

25 **Making the Second Layer**

ANIMATING WITH SCALE

As well as moving an object or objects from one position to another, motion tweening can be used to vary the size of an object. Follow the simple instructions below to create an eye-catching animated flying heading.

1 CREATING TEXT TO ANIMATE

● Open a new Flash movie. Type in a short phrase as a single line of text near one corner of the stage. Choose the font face, color, and style in the **Character** Panel.

● Right mouse click in frame 12 to access the Frame menu.

● Choose **Insert Keyframe**.

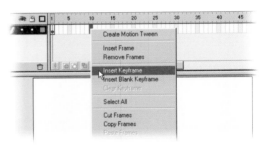

● With the new keyframe selected, use the **Arrow** tool to drag the text to the opposite corner of the stage.

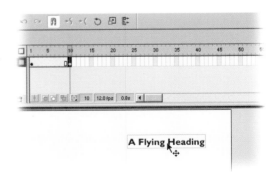

2 SCALING THE TEXT

● Make sure that the **Arrow** tool is selected in the toolbox, the text is selected on the stage, and the second keyframe is selected in the timeline.

● Click on the **Scale** option in the toolbox.

● Drag the text from a corner marker to enlarge it.

3 CREATING THE TWEEN

● Right mouse click in any of the frames between one and 12 to access the **Frame** menu.

● Choose **Create Motion Tween**.

● Play the animation using [Enter ←] (on the keyboard) or the **Controller**. The text will fly up the stage and enlarge smoothly.

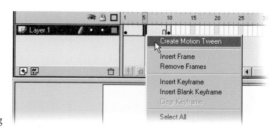

USING THE CONTROLLER

There is a **Controller** toolbar, which is useful when you are working on animations. Go to **Window** and choose **Toolbars**, then **Controller** from the drop-down menu. You will access a window with playback controls including **Stop**, **Rewind**, **Play**, and **Go To End**. You can also **Step Forward** and **Step Back** one frame at a time.

RECYCLING GRAPHICS

When you convert a piece of artwork into a symbol, as well as enabling Flash to make a Motion Tween, you are turning it into a form that can be used more than once in a movie. As you make symbols, you are building up a library of objects that you can bring onto the stage again and again without adding to the file size.

USING SYMBOLS FROM YOUR LIBRARY

Each time a symbol appears on the stage, it is known as an "instance" and can be modified without changing the original symbol. This example has graphics on three layers in frame one: a background design, a round-edged rectangle with a solid fill that will make a button, and a heading that contains a single line of text.

1 CREATING A SYMBOL

● Select the buttons layer in the timeline and the rectangle graphic on the stage.
● Use F8 as a keyboard shortcut to bring up the **Symbol Properties** box.
● Name the symbol and select the **Graphic** option.

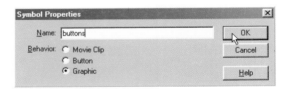

2 USING THE LIBRARY

● Go to **Window** and choose **Library** from the drop-down menu. This accesses the movie's **Library** window.

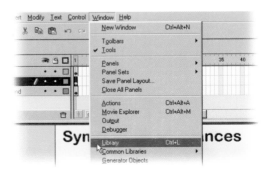

● There is only one graphic in the library, which is the one that has just been created.

● Select its name and it will be displayed in the library window.

● With the button layer selected in the timeline, drag the symbol from the library window to the stage.

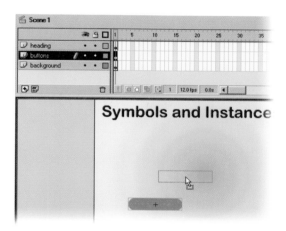

Symbol appears in library window ●

● Drag more instances onto the stage until you have four of them.

3 MODIFYING INSTANCES

● Select one of the instances, choose **Scale** from the **Options** in the toolbox, and resize this version of the button.

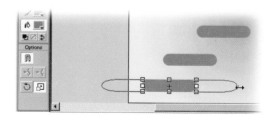

CREATING MOTION GUIDES

When you apply a Motion Tween between two graphics in different positions on the stage, Flash creates movement along the straight line that joins them. Sometimes, however, you will want to animate an object along a curved or uneven path.

To do this, you create a Motion Path layer and draw the line that the animated graphic will follow. The example here has a background layer called scenery and a layer containing a balloon that has been drawn off stage in the **Work Area**.

1 PREPARING THE ANIMATION

● Convert the artwork into a symbol with **Graphic** behavior and name it ⬜.
● Insert a frame in frame 24 of the background layer so that it will display for two seconds.

● Make a second keyframe in the balloon layer at frame 24.
● Use the **Arrow** tool to move the graphic to the other side of the stage in the second keyframe.
● Select **Scale** from the toolbox options and make the balloon smaller.
● Create a **Motion Tween** between the two keyframes.
● Play the animation – the balloon will drift away over the scenery. Note that it would look better if the balloon drifted along a curved rather than a straight path.

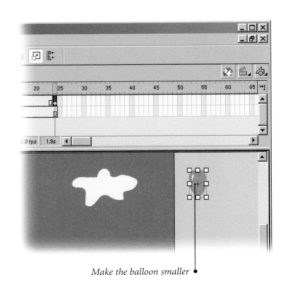

Make the balloon smaller ●

⬜ 44 **Creating a Symbol**

2 ADDING THE MOTION GUIDE

● Right mouse click on the **Layer Name** bar of the balloon layer.

● Choose **Add Motion Guide** from the menu.

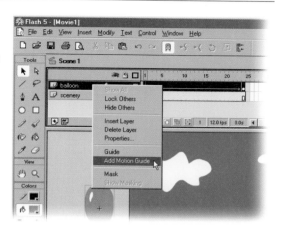

● Pick up the **Pencil** tool ⌐ from the toolbox, select **Smooth** in the **Options** ⌐ section of the toolbox, and draw a gentle, meandering path for the balloon to follow, starting at the center point of the balloon in frame one.

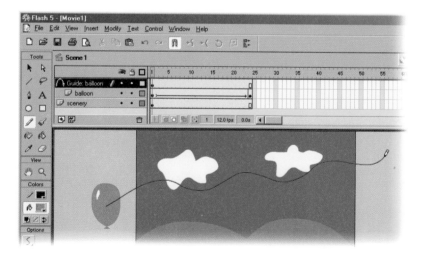

16 ❶ Tools   16 ❹ Options

● Select the second keyframe in the balloon layer and use the **Arrow** tool from the toolbox to drag the graphic to the end of the line. It will snap into place.

● Play the animation. The balloon will now follow the path.

● If the balloon does not follow its motion guide, check that the graphic is snapped to the line in the first and the last keyframe.

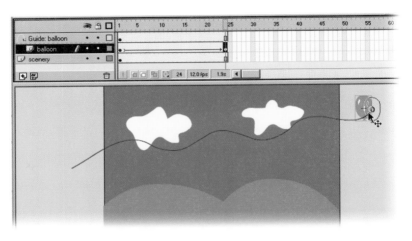

3 HIDING THE GUIDE

● The **Motion Guide** should not display in the animation, and, like the grid on the stage, will not be visible when you publish the movie.

● If you want to see the animation in Flash without the guide line, then switch off the visibility of the **Guide** layer by clicking on the dot below the eye symbol in the **Layer Name** bar.

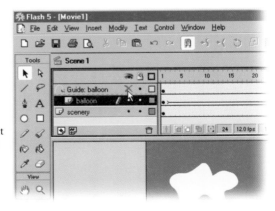

4 ORIENT TO PATH DIRECTION

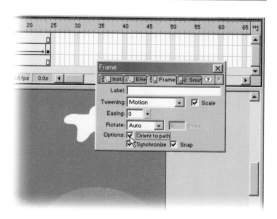

● You can make the balloon move more naturally on the path by orienting it to the direction of the path.

● Go to **Window** and choose **Panels**, then **Frame**.

● Put a check mark on the **Orient to path** in the **Frame** panel.

● Close the **Frame** panel and play the animation. The balloon will follow the direction and angle of the path.

THERE ARE MORE WAYS THAN ONE

Flash usually offers you several ways of doing the same thing. Let's look at inserting a new layer into the timeline as an example. You can go to **Insert** and choose **Layer** from the drop-down menu, or right-click in the **Layer Name** bar and choose **Insert Layer**, or click on the **Insert Layer** icon on the bottom left of the timeline. When inserting a keyframe, you can select the relevant frame, go to **Insert**, and choose **Keyframe** from the menu, or right mouse click in the frame to access the **Insert** menu and choose **Insert Keyframe**, or use the keyboard shortcut F6.

Multiple Effects

You can apply more than one type of Tween at a time to your Flash movie. So, if you wish, you can animate an object to fade and scale, or move and rotate at the same time, or, indeed, all three effects can be applied at once.

LOCKING A LAYER

If you have work in a layer that you do not want to edit or move accidentally – for example, in a background that needs to stay unchanged throughout an animation – you can lock the layer by clicking **Lock Layer** in the **Layer Name** bar.

When the layer is locked, the **Lock Layer** spot becomes a lock icon.

INTRODUCING SOUND

To make your animations even more innovative, try introducing sounds into your movies. Flash lets you coordinate sounds with events in a movie by placing a sound in a keyframe. This example animates the word FLASH with sound.

1 PREPARING THE ANIMATED TEXT

● Make two layers in the timeline in a new Flash movie. Call one layer **Flash** and the other **Sounds**.
● In frame one of the Flash layer, type in a big, bright **F**. Remember that you can change its font size, color, and face in the **Character** panel ▯.

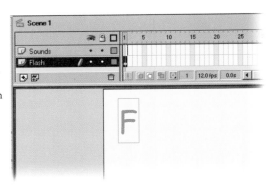

● Insert a keyframe into frame two of the Flash layer. It will already contain the F from frame one, so type an **L**.
● Make a new keyframe for the **A**, then the **S**, then the **H**, until you have the word **FLASH** in the keyframe at frame five.
● Play the animation. The letters appear on the stage one at a time.

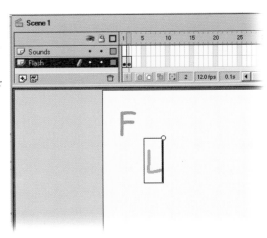

2 OPENING THE SOUND LIBRARY

● Go to **Window** and choose **Common Libraries** and then **Sounds** from the drop-down menus to access the **Sounds Library**.

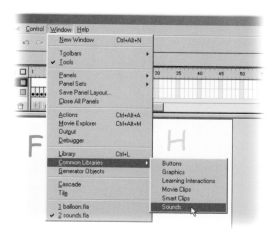

● Select a sound from the list and press the play button in the **Library** window to hear it.

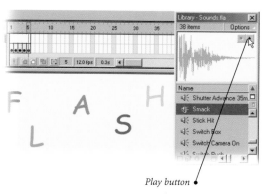

Play button ●

3 ADDING SOUND TO THE MOVIE

● Select frame one of the **Sounds** layer in the timeline.
● Drag a sound from the **Sounds Library** onto the stage.

● Make frame two of the
Sounds layer a keyframe.
● Drag another sound
from the library onto
the stage in the second
keyframe.

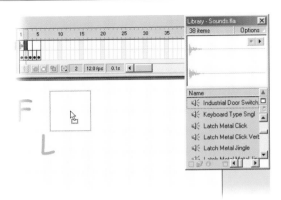

● Make each of the five
frames a keyframe and drag
a new sound onto the stage
from the library.
● Note the sound wave
displaying in each of the
frames.
● Play the movie. As each
letter appears on the stage,
there will be a sound.

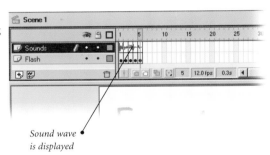

*Sound wave
is displayed*

COORDINATING SOUND AND ANIMATION

This example of sound
introduction into a
Flash movie is a frame-
by-frame animation.
However, it is just
as straightforward to
coordinate sounds and
images in tweened
animation. To do this,
keep your sound in a
separate layer, insert a
keyframe at the point in the
frame where you want the
sound to begin, and,
finally, drag your chosen
sound onto the stage.

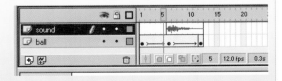

SHAPE TWEENING

You can make shapes and colors morph from one to another with a Shape Tween. Unlike Motion Tweening, you must be able to edit the graphics that you are morphing, so you must not convert your graphic into a symbol to make a Shape Tween.

1 CREATING TWO SHAPES

● Draw a circle without a stroke outline in one corner of the stage. To switch off the stroke for the **Oval** tool, click on **Stroke Color** in the toolbox and select the white box with a red line through it – this represents no color.

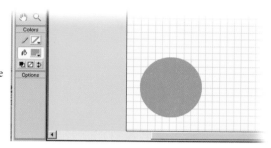

● Right mouse click in frame ten and choose **Insert Blank Keyframe**. This makes a keyframe that contains no artwork; a standard keyframe here would contain a red circle.

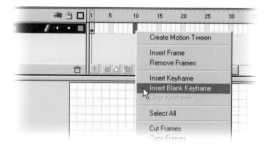

● Change the **Fill Color** and draw a star in the opposite corner of the stage, using the **Pen** tool.

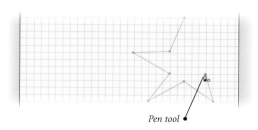

Pen tool ●

● Both shapes should not have an outline. Select the star's stroke by double clicking on it with the **Arrow** tool, and press Del on the keyboard.

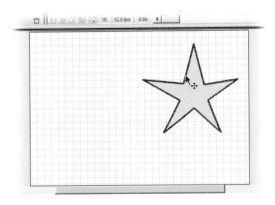

2 MAKING THE SHAPE TWEEN

● Click between the keyframes in the timeline to select the intervening frames.
● Go to **Window** and choose **Panels**, then **Frame** from the drop-down menu to access the **Frame** panel.

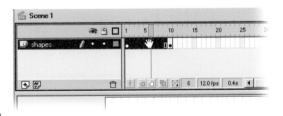

● Choose **Shape** from the **Tweening** drop-down menu.
● Leave **Easing** and **Blend** at their default settings.
● Close the **Frame** Panel and play your animation. The circle will morph into the star over ten frames. If it works too fast, double click on the frame rate in the timeline to access the **Movie Properties** box and reduce the frame rate.

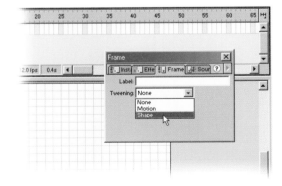

3 TESTING THE MOVIE

● Go to **Control** and choose **Test Movie** from the drop-down menu.

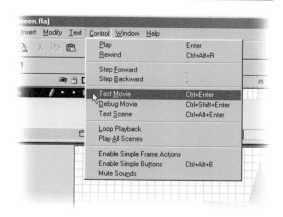

● Flash plays a preview of the movie as it will look when published. Note that the grid is not showing and that **Loop Playback** is the default setting.

● Go to **File** and choose **Close** from the drop-down menu that appears. This does not close the Flash movie file itself – only the movie preview.

FLASH INTERACTIVITY

While animation is central to the appeal of Flash, another strength lies in its ability to produce more complex interactivity than HTML-based web pages offer.

WHAT IS INTERACTIVITY?

The animations that you have produced so far have been linear, playing from start to end, and stopping or looping. However, a visitor to a Flashed web site would expect interactivity, which would allow them to take alternative paths through your movie. To create this interactivity, you need to stop the movie playing at a frame that contains buttons linked to other parts of the movie.

ACTION SCRIPTING

These links are created using Flash's Action Scripting, a programming language similar to JavaScript. Fortunately, you do not need to be a programmer to use Action Scripts, as you enter values into an Actions window and Flash does all the work.

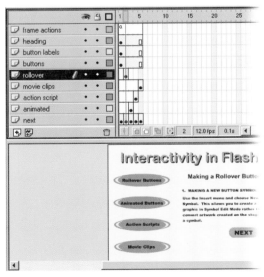

CREATING A ROLLOVER BUTTON

Buttons, known as rollover buttons, are central to generating interactivity in a Flash movie. If a button on a movie screen is clickable, you will see that it changes its appearance as the mouse rolls over the button.

1 MAKING A NEW BUTTON SYMBOL

● Go to **Insert** and choose **New Symbol** from the drop-down menu.
● This allows you to create a graphic in **Symbol Edit Mode** rather than convert artwork on the stage into a symbol.

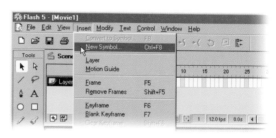

● Select **Button** from **Behavior** options. Name the button and then click **OK** to enter **Button Symbol Edit Mode**.

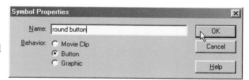

2 BUTTON SYMBOL EDIT MODE

● The timeline has four important frames: **Up** (this is how the button will look before the mouse pointer rolls over it); **Over** (this is the appearance of the button when the mouse rolls over it), **Down** (when the mouse is clicked on the button), and **Hit** (where the button is active).

3 CREATING FOUR BUTTON STATES

● Draw a button at the center of the stage over the crosshair. This is the **Up** state of the button – or how the button will look initially.

● Right mouse click in the **Over** frame and select **Insert Keyframe**.
● There is now a copy of the **Over** graphic in this new keyframe. Press [Esc] on the keyboard to deselect.

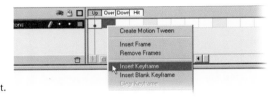

● Pick a new **Fill Color** and fill the graphic.
● Right mouse click in the **Down** frame and select **Insert Keyframe**.
● Change the **Fill Color** of this copy of the button.
● Right mouse click in the **Hit** frame and select **Insert Keyframe**.
● This graphic will not appear in the movie, so there is no need to edit it. The **Hit** state confines the active area when you apply Actions later.
● Click on **Scene 1** to return to the movie.

Click on Scene 1 ●

4 ADDING BUTTON TO THE MOVIE

● Go to **Window** and select **Library** from the drop-down menu to access the movie's **Library** window.

● Select the button that you have just made in the library window.

● Drag an instance of the button onto the stage.

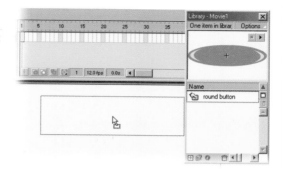

5 TESTING THE BUTTON

● Go to **Control** and select **Enable Simple Buttons** from the drop-down menu.

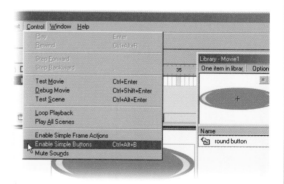

● Rollover and click on the button to test it.

● Go to **Control** and uncheck **Enable Simple Buttons** from the drop-down menu – this will disable the button on stage.

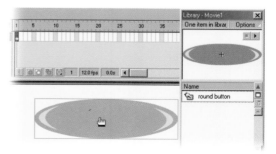

ADDING ACTIONS TO BUTTONS

You have learned how to give buttons rollover effects, but not yet how to make a button link to another part of your movie. You can instruct a button to link to another frame in the timeline through an Action Script applied to the button, or an Object Action, but this poses a problem. If there is more than one frame in the timeline, Flash will try to send the playhead through the movie. To make a movie stand still until a mouse is clicked on a button, you have to instruct Flash to stop with another Action Script, this time a Frame Action. This example is the simplest type of interactive movie you can make, and is a good starting point for learning about Action Scripting. It features the button that you have just made, plus one other.

1 PREPARING THE BUTTONS

● Make another new button in **Symbol Edit Mode**. We are calling this one **box button**.
● Give **Layer 1** the name **Buttons**.
● Right mouse click in frame two and choose **Insert Blank Keyframe** ⌐.
● Drag the new button onto the stage from the library window into this new keyframe.

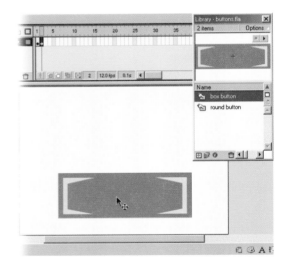

● Pull the **Playhead** back
to frame one.
● The first button that we
made is on the stage in
frame one.
● Close the **Library**
window.

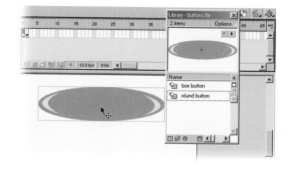

2 ADDING A STOP FRAME ACTION

● Add a **New Layer** to the
timeline, insert a frame at
frame two, and name the
layer **frame actions**.

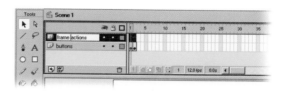

● With frame one in the
frame actions layer selected,
go to **Window** and choose
Actions from the drop-
down menu.

● Note that the **Actions**
window specifies **Frame
Actions** on its blue bar.
● Click on the plus (+)
sign and choose **Stop** from
the **Basic Actions** menu.

● The stop action (**stop O**) is now in the code window on the right, and there is a small letter "**a**" displayed in frame one of the **frame actions** layer. This shows an action has been applied to that frame.

● The stop frame action also applies to frame two, because you inserted a frame into frame two before applying the action.

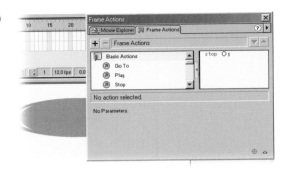

3 ADDING AN OBJECT ACTION

● To add an object action to the first button, click on the button in frame one.

● Notice the **Actions** window now specifies **Object Actions** because you have an object selected.

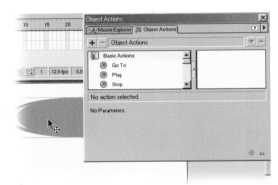

● Drag **Go To** from the left window to the right.

● The **Go To** action code created by Flash in the right window is automatically set to **On Release**, so the movie will go to a new frame when the mouse is clicked and released.

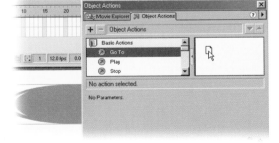

● To specify the frame that the movie will jump to, type **2** into the **Frame** field at the bottom of the **Basic Actions** window.

● Uncheck **Go To** and **Play**, and the frame will become **Go To** and **Stop** in the Action Scripting.

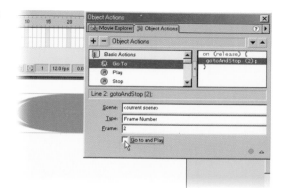

● To add an object action to the second button, pull the playhead to frame two in the timeline.

● Select the button in this frame by clicking on it with the **Arrow** tool.

● When the button is selected, the **Action** window will specify **Object Actions**.

● Double click on **Go To** in the **Object Actions** window.

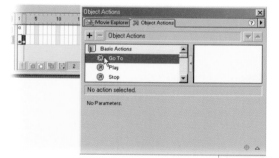

● This time, the Action will need to jump the movie back to frame one, so leave **1** in the **Frame** field.

● Uncheck **Go to and Play**.

● Use the **Control** menu and choose **Test Movie**.

● When the movie preview comes up on the screen, you should note the first button. Click on it, and you will see the second button, which you should click on.

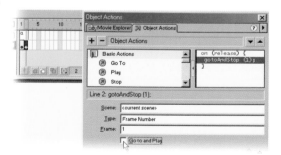

Movies On The Web

Flash allows you to export a finished project in a variety of movie and still-image formats. The most useful one prepares your Flash movie for publication on the web.

Playing Flash Movies on the Web

You have so far been saving your movies in Flash's own format, with the file extension **.fla**. This format can only be read by Flash, so it is not useful for showing your finished work or putting movies on the web. To play movies on the web, you need the Shockwave Flash format, which uses the file extension **.swf**.

FLASH PLAYER

If you have embedded a Shockwave Flash movie into a web page, or made a whole website in Flash, a visitor to your site who has an older version of a browser will need to have the Flash Player program. This can be downloaded from the internet for free from **Macromedia.com**. To make this easy for visitors to your site, you could add a link to the Macromedia website on the first page of your movie for people who do not have the plug-in.

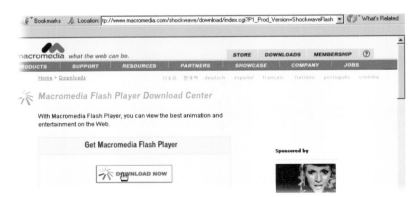

TESTING THE PERFORMANCE

When a Flash movie plays on the web, it starts playing the first frames before the subsequent frames have been downloaded. This is known as streaming, and it means that the movie can start to play quickly. However, if the rest of the movie takes longer to download than it does to play, then the movie will have to pause and wait for the next frames to catch up. You can test the performance of your movie to check the likelihood of this happening on a range of internet connection speeds.

1 CHOOSING A CONNECTION

● When you have finished a Flash movie, go to **Control** and select **Test Movie** from the drop-down menu.
● In preview mode, go to **Debug** and choose a modem speed from the drop-down menu.
● A 56K modem is currently the most common in domestic use.

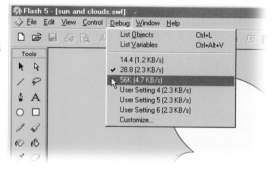

2 TESTING THE PERFORMANCE

● Go to **View** and choose **Bandwidth Profiler** from the drop-down menu.

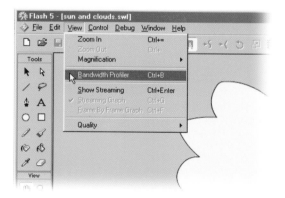

● The bar chart displays information on the movie frame by frame. If the bar for a particular frame is higher than the red line, the movie cannot stream fast enough at the selected connection speed to play the movie without pausing.
● To finish, close the chart and the movie test.

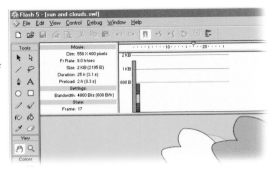

CHECKING THE PUBLISH SETTINGS

Flash has a Publish export function, which prepares not just the Shockwave Flash file of your movie, but also the HTML (Hypertext Markup Language) file in which the Flash movie will sit in order to play in a browser.

1 SETTING THE FORMATS
● Go to **File** and choose **Publish Settings**.
● Click on the **Formats** tab. Under **Type**, check **Flash** (**.swf**) and **HTML** (**.html**)
● Under **filenames**, uncheck **Use default names**.
● This allows you to change the filenames of your movie and your HTML documents. If the movie is the first page of a web site, you should name your HTML file index because that is usually the filename loaded first by default in a web site.

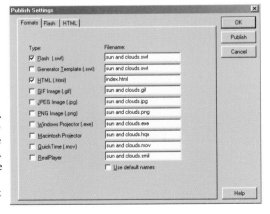

2 SETTING THE HTML

● Click on the **HTML** tab.
● The default setting for the **Dimensions** of the movie is **Match Movie**, which will display the movie at the pixel dimensions of the stage. If you want the movie to fill the browser window, change that setting to **Percent** and see that the **Width** and **Height** are both set to **100**.
● The default **Quality** is set to **High**, but if your movie failed its performance test, you could try dropping the quality to lose some file size.

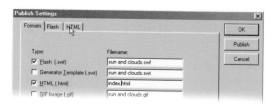

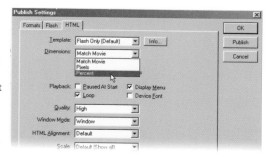

3 THE FLASH SETTINGS

● Click on the **Flash** tab.
● The **Load Order** is set to **Bottom up**, so that the lowest frames in the time-line will be loaded first.
● The JPEG quality is particularly important if you have imported photos into your movie. The higher the quality, the larger the file size, so experiment with the settings to see how low you can take the slider without losing image quality. You will see how to preview your publish settings in the next step.

PUBLISHING FOR THE WEB

Before you actually publish your Flash movie for the web, you will want to check how it looks in a web browser. Flash offers you the facility to do this within the program by following a sequence of menus, as shown here.

1 PREVIEWING AS A WEB PAGE

● Go to **File** and choose **Publish Preview**, then **Default – (HTML) F12** from the drop-down menu.
● The movie then loads into a web browser.

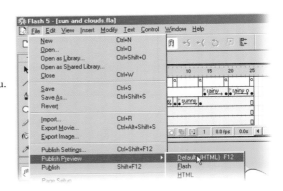

2 PUBLISHING THE FLASH MOVIE

● If you are happy with the Flash movie as it appears in the web page, go to **File** and choose **Publish** from the drop-down menu. Flash creates the **.swf** and **.html** files. These are now ready to upload to the internet.

PUBLISHING THE PROJECT AS A STAND-ALONE MOVIE

You may want to publish your project as a stand-alone movie, which is known as a "projector."

In the **Formats** tab of the **Publish Settings** box, place a check mark on **Windows Projector (.exe)** before you

publish. Double click on the **.exe** file where you saved it, and it will launch and run without a browser.

EXPORTING A MOVIE

Publishing for the web is not always the right method to use for exporting. If you use Flash to make an animated banner for a web page built in Dreamweaver, you will want to export your Flash project as an **.swf** file and embed it into your web page.

1 EXPORTING AS AN .SWF FILE

● Go to the **File** menu and choose **Export Movie** from the drop-down menu.

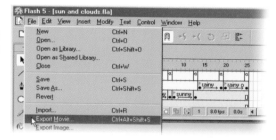

● Navigate to the folder in which you want to save your movie, name it, and then click on **Save**.

● You are then offered the **Export Flash Player** settings box, which is similar to the **Flash** tab in the **Publish Settings** box. Choose your settings and click on **OK** to save the movie as a "Shockwave" file in the chosen folder ready for uploading.

GLOSSARY

ACTION SCRIPT
The programming language, similar to JavaScript, that Flash uses to create interactivity.

BLANK KEYFRAME
A keyframe that has no content, leaving the stage empty in that particular frame.

BUTTON
A graphic that can be clicked on.

BUTTON STATE
The appearance of a button may be different before a mouse rolls over, as the mouse rolls over it, and when the mouse is clicked. Each of these is a Button State.

DOWN STATE
The appearance of a button when the mouse clicks on it.

EXPORT
To output a publishable version of a Flash movie.

FRAME RATE
The number of frames per second at which an animation plays.

FRAME-BY-FRAME ANIMATION
Animation in which every frame is a keyframe and there is no Tweening.

HIT STATE
The area of a button that responds to a click.

HTML (HYPERTEXT MARKUP LANGUAGE)
The code that web pages are written in. Web browsers interpret HTML code to display text, images, and other web content.

IMPORT
Bringing into a movie a file that was not created in Flash.

INSTANCE
When a Symbol from the Library is on the Stage, it is an Instance of that Symbol. You can have numerous Instances of the same Symbol on the Stage at the same time.

KEYFRAME
A frame in which a major change occurs.

LAYER
Like a stack of sheets of transparent acetate, layers are a way of organizing your artwork.

LIBRARY
Each Flash movie develops a Library of Symbols, elements that have been used in that movie.

MOTION GUIDE
A layer that contains a line along which a Motion Tweened object can move.

MOTION TWEEN
An animation created between two keyframes that are not adjacent and that contain a graphic in different positions, or with different qualities.

MOVIE CLIP
A Symbol that can act as a movie within a movie. A Movie Clip Symbol has its own timeline, but the animation created in it can be placed in one frame of the movie, where it resides.

OVER STATE
The appearance of a button when a mouse rolls over it.

PUBLISH
To export a movie that is to be put on the web or played as a stand-alone movie.

ROLLOVER BUTTON
A button that responds to a mouse rolling over it.

SHAPE TWEEN
An animation that creates a morph between two shapes, so that the first shape changes progressively into the second.

STAGE
The white area at the center of the Flash interface where a movie is displayed.

SYMBOL
All elements that are used in a movie are stored as Symbols in the Library.

TIMELINE
The part of the Flash screen on which a movie's Frames, Keyframes, and Layers are displayed.

TWEENING
Automated animation function, in which Flash fills in the frames between two keyframes at the start and end of an animated sequence.

UP STATE
The appearance of a button before a mouse rolls over it.

INDEX

ACKNOWLEDGMENTS

PUBLISHER'S ACKNOWLEDGMENTS
Dorling Kindersley would like to thank the following:
Paul Mattock of APM, Brighton, for commissioned photography.

Screen shots of Macromedia® Flash® used
by permission from Macromedia Inc.

*Every effort has been made to trace the copyright holders.
The publisher apologizes for any unintentional omissions and would be pleased,
in such cases, to place an acknowledgment in future editions of this book.*

All other images © Dorling Kindersley.
For further information see: www.dkimages.com